21st
Century
Skills Library

HEALTH AT RISK

DRUGS

Toney Allman

Cherry Lake Publishing
Ann Arbor, Michigan

Cherry Lake
Publishing

Published in the United States of America by Cherry Lake Publishing
Ann Arbor, Michigan
www.cherrylakepublishing.com

Content Advisor: Carolyn Walker, RN, PhD, Professor, School of Nursing, San Diego State University, San Diego, California

Photo Credits: Cover and page 1, Alamy; page 4, © Radius Images/Alamy; page 6, © fl online/Alamy; page 7, © Picture Partners/Alamy; page 9, © Itani/Alamy; page 11, © Cleo Photo/Alamy; page 13, © Janine Weidel/Alamy; page 15, © Janine Weidel/Alamy; page 17, © Itani/Alamy; page 18, © David M. Grossman/Alamy; page 20, Alamy; page 22, © David M. Grossman/Alamy; page 24, © Mike Goldwater/Alamy; page 25, © Heather Gail Delaney/Alamy; page 26, © Jeff Greenberg/Alamy; page 28, AP Images/Chris Carlson

Library of Congress Cataloging-in-Publication Data
Allman, Toney.
Drugs / Toney Allman
    p. cm.— (Health at Risk)
Includes index.
ISBN-13: 978-1-60279-283-8
ISBN-10: 1-60279-283-6
1. Substance abuse—Juvenile literature. I. Title.
RC564.3.F73 2008
616.86—dc22   2008017503

Cherry Lake Publishing would like to acknowledge the work of
The Partnership for 21st Century Skills.
Please visit www.21stcenturyskills.org for more information.

TABLE of CONTENTS

CHAPTER ONE

WHAT'S THE BIG DEAL ABOUT DRUGS?

Taking drugs can sometimes seem like a quick hit to feel better or release stress, but it leads to more problems.

Krystan didn't think trying drugs was a big deal. She was 10 years old and living in California when she saw her older brother smoking marijuana, often called pot or weed. She thought it would be fun and convinced him to let her try it. She felt cool. At age 13, she tried methamphetamine, also called speed or meth. Then she added cocaine, LSD, and so-called magic mushrooms. By age 16, she stopped caring about school, sports, or friends. She didn't remember to eat. She became really skinny. She got in fights and stole to buy drugs. She says she began to feel like a monster.

Doing drugs might seem fun at first. But drug abusers know that it stops

Some experts think marijuana should be a legal drug. They say it can help people who suffer pain or discomfort from sicknesses such as AIDS or cancer. Other experts say there is no proof marijuana can help these people. They believe other, legal drugs can be used instead. Search the Web or your library to find different points of view on the debate over medical marijuana. List the arguments on both sides of the issue. Which arguments do you think are stronger? Why?

Pot remains a popular first drug among teens.

being fun. Some kids don't like to hear this. They want to feel what it's like to get high for themselves. In 2007, 19 percent of 8th graders in the United States had tried **recreational drugs** at least once. These include drugs such as pot, meth, LSD, and cocaine. About 36 percent of 10th graders and 47 percent of 12th graders have tried one of these types of drugs. In Canada, about one-third of kids report trying pot. One in 20 Canadian teens reports using other illegal drugs.

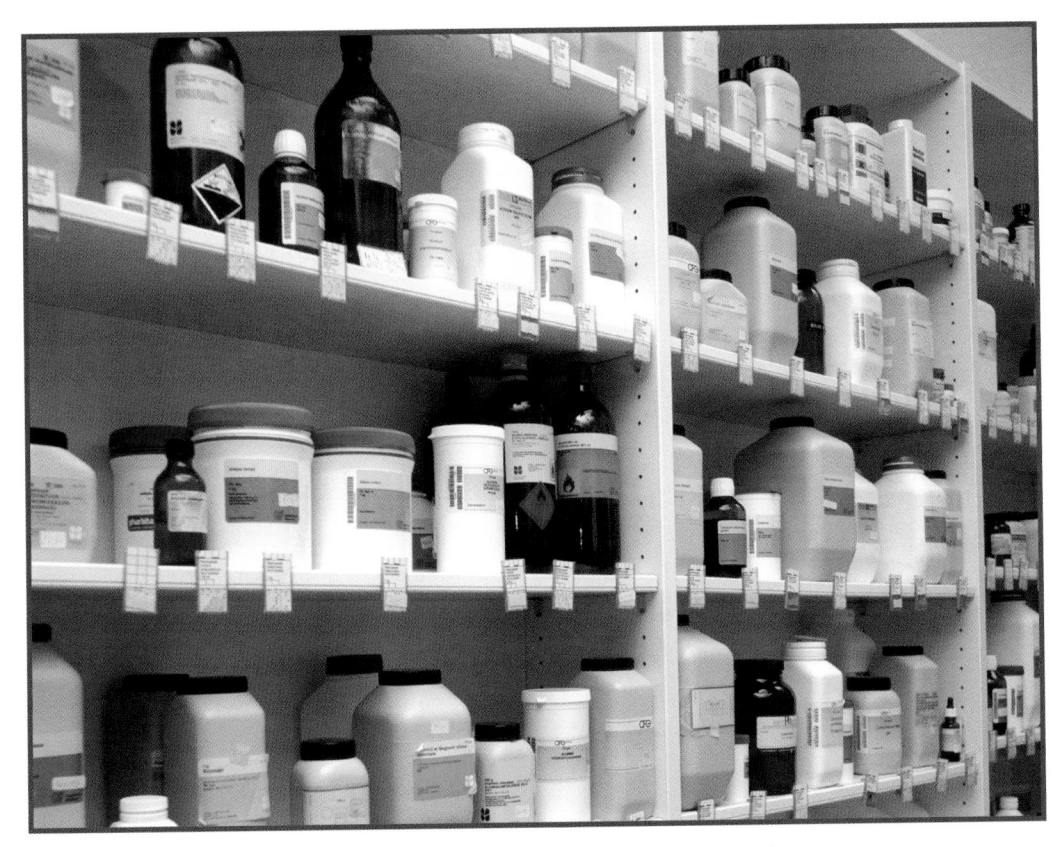

Prescription drugs may be the first drugs kids try because they are easy to steal from the family medicine chest.

Recreational drugs are illegal. Illegal drugs can also be called street drugs. Street drugs are not the only unsafe drugs used to get high.

Some young people experiment with **prescription drugs**. These are drugs ordered by doctors for someone

with a specific medical need. Sometimes kids sneak these drugs from their parents. They think the drugs must be safe because they are legal. But they are only safe for the person who is supposed to take them. They are not safe for other people.

Some kids try **over-the-counter drugs**, too. These are products you can buy without a prescription. Kids swallow cold tablets or cough syrup. The Center for Parent/Youth Understanding is a family support organization in Canada. It did a survey in 2007. It found that one in 10 of Canada's teens drank cough syrup to get high. This is a problem because no kind of **drug abuse** is safe.

CHAPTER TWO

THE HARM DRUGS CAUSE

A teen is rarely ready to face the many consequences that drug use may bring, including the effects such drugs have on the mind and body.

Drug abuse hurts bodies and minds. Getting high changes how you feel and how you act. You can't think clearly and you might make bad decisions. Getting high also affects your body's normal functions. The high wears off and you feel bad or sick unless you take more of the drug. Your body needs it. This is called **addiction**. Some people who are addicted to drugs will do anything to get them.

Eric was in high school and living in South Dakota when he became addicted to meth. This meant his body needed the drug. Meth mimics certain chemicals in the brain. These chemicals make people feel pleasure.

Some drugs, such as meth, are highly addictive.
Addiction can lead to obsession, where the only thought
is how and where to get more of the drug.

After a while, Eric's brain couldn't make its own pleasure chemicals. Meth suppressed them. His brain was starved for those pleasure feelings. He took more meth, but his body was too used to it. He couldn't get enough and felt bad all the time.

Meth poisoned Eric's life. He dropped out of school. He stole money from his mom to get drugs. He lived in the street, homeless and lonely. That's the problem with many illegal drugs. Even if you want to stop, you can't. The drug takes over your life.

Other drugs may not be physically addictive. But they are still harmful to your health. For instance, cough syrups and cold medicines are poisons if taken in large doses. The ingredient **DXM** acts like a depressant, or downer, on the central nervous system. The central nervous system includes the brain, the spinal cord, and nerves. Depressants slow down the central nervous system.

Teens face many pressures in school and in life that can sometimes seem unbearable. Taking drugs rarely leads to a happier life, however.

They can even put it to sleep. Users feel drunk and may **hallucinate**. People who take too much can't move their arms and legs. They can't talk. Their breathing slows. They may suffer brain damage or even die. The trouble is that when you experiment, you never know how much is too much.

Anyone who abuses drugs is taking a chance. Taking drugs illegally can damage your health, your schoolwork, your friendships, your family, and your future.

CHAPTER THREE

WHY PEOPLE GET HIGH

A teen may be more likely to experiment with drugs if his or her friends are also experimenting. Some drugs make people stop caring about fun or meaningful activities.

Young people try drugs for lots of different reasons. Sometimes they want to be like other kids. Sometimes they are unhappy. They think getting high will make them feel

better. Sometimes, they just want to know what it feels like to get high. Curious teens try lots of new things, especially if they think they are safe.

In 2007, Partnership for a Drug-Free America reported a survey of teens. Forty percent of teens thought they were safer getting high on prescription drugs than street drugs. This is not true. Carl Hennon of Ohio thought he was safe when he used prescription painkillers and cough syrup to get high. His drug-using friends told him the drugs were safe. He found Internet sites that talked about how to use the drugs. He experimented and enjoyed friendships with other users. But one morning in 2003, his mom found him dead in his bed. He died of a drug overdose. He was 18 years old.

Dave grew up in Monroe, New York. He wasn't thinking about drug safety when he first got high. He just wanted to know

Taking large quantities of medicines such as cough syrup may seem fairly harmless, but even these drugs can become dangerous.

what it felt like. He first smoked pot at a party. He was 15 years old at the time. He says he wasn't pressured into it. He wasn't trying to fit in with the other kids. He was just curious. But drug use became a habit. After a while, he couldn't get along without smoking pot every day.

Feeling isolated and alone is a common feeling during adolescence and early adulthood. Other teens must face more serious problems, such as a parent who is an alcoholic or sexual abuse. Such pressures may make drugs even more appealing.

Some kids look to drugs as an escape. Megan Hakeman was 13 years old when she first tried drugs. She was being sexually abused at the time. She thought getting high would help her forget her problems. She started with pot and then began **huffing**. She inhaled vapors from household products like air fresheners and cleaners. But huffing has serious health risks. Using drugs to cope with one problem just caused a new problem.

People use drugs to feel good, but the good feelings don't last. Eventually, they feel worse. They want to stop abusing drugs and get back in control of their lives.

21st Century Content

According to Partnership for a Drug-Free America, 98 percent of movies show people abusing drugs or alcohol. Rap songs mention substance abuse 75 percent of the time. Almost half of all teens say that movies and TV make it seem okay to use drugs. Young people need to learn how to analyze these drug messages. The U.S. Department of Health and Human Services suggests that you ask these questions when you hear a media message that makes drugs seem fun:

What is the message maker's point of view?

How does the message make you feel?

What special words, images, and sounds are used to create the message?

Who created the message and why?

CHAPTER FOUR

BEATING DRUG ABUSE

Direct confrontation from a friend or family member can sometimes help an addicted or drug using teen to realize that his or her addiction is out of control.

Beating drug abuse isn't easy, but it can be done. First you have to admit that your life is out of control. And then you have to want help.

One girl posted her story about beating drug abuse on Partnership for a Drug-Free America's blog. She said her parents helped her help herself by being tough. They had her tested for drugs every couple of weeks. Her mom made her stop going to parties and drop her drug-using friends. This girl thinks her mother did the right thing. She has made new friends and feels sorry for the old ones who are still messing up their lives.

Krystan's parents supported her, too. When she was 17, her mom searched her backpack and found her meth pipe. Her mother forced Krystan to go to counseling. The counselor told Krystan to ask for help or leave the office. Krystan

Drug counselors work with people who have drug problems. They work in many settings. Drug users often get into trouble with the law. So counselors may work in juvenile detention centers or **halfway houses**. Or, they may work in hospitals, homeless shelters, or welfare agencies.

Drug counselors try to help drug users face their problems. They try to guide users in making changes in their lives. Most drug counselors complete college degrees. Many are also licensed and certified by the state in which they work.

Drug addiction is a serious problem that must be treated with the help of professionals.

was going to leave, but somehow she asked for help instead. The counselor got Krystan into a **drug treatment center** for 30 days. She lived there with other addicts and couldn't get any drugs. This gave her time to get over her addiction. Then Krystan moved into a halfway house for another 30 days. She lived in this group home while she got used to normal life without drugs. She got support and counseling. It was hard, but Krystan stayed clean. She has been drug-free for eight years.

Dave realized that pot was hurting him. He was smoking it every day. He sought help in a treatment center. Many of his friends didn't believe he was

21st Century Content

Many schools have a zero-tolerance policy for drugs. This means that drugs are not allowed on school grounds, period. Students caught with drugs in any amount may be suspended or expelled. No warnings are given. Excuses are not accepted. Find out what kind of drug policy your school has. Do you think the policy is fair? Why or why not?

Teens can turn their lives around after addiction, but but therapy and counseling take hard work.

addicted. They thought pot was safe. But Dave listened to the former drug abusers at the center. They taught him not to listen to his old friends. Dave says drug abusers need to admit their problems and find a better way to live.

CHAPTER FIVE

HOW NOT TO USE DRUGS

Teens can rarely change their addictive behaviors on their own. Adults must step in to help.

The best way to avoid drug abuse is never to try drugs in the first place. Knowing the facts about drugs is a good start.

Some anti-drug programs in the schools have had great success in helping kids to avoid drugs in the first place.

Speakers from the Narconon drug prevention program have visited many schools. Over the years, they have talked to more than 1.5 million students. Many of the speakers were once drug users. They share real stories of the pain they suffered. They talk about the harm drugs cause.

Surveys of students who take part in Narconon programs show that they get the message. More than 90 percent of the students say the talks have taught them a lot about drugs. One student said, "I thought about trying pot out of curiosity, but now I'm afraid [be]cause of how it will harm you. There's no point." Another explained, "My thoughts about drugs had changed. I used to think drugs were cool. I thought since everybody does it, I should do it, too. Now I realize that drugs are bad." The more kids know, says Narconon, the less likely they are to try drugs.

Lots of drug prevention programs try to get good information to kids. In Canada, one program works with indigenous, or native, peoples. Kids

Life & Career Skills

A friend or even a stranger might one day offer you drugs. If that happens, how will you respond? Partnership for a Drug-Free America suggests answers like these:

- "No, thanks. I'm not into that."
- "Nah, I'm in training for —."
- "No. I gotta go in a bit."
- "No, thanks. I don't like how it makes people not act like themselves."

What other answers could you give?

A surf instructor teaches a class of inner-city youths how to surf.
Meaningful activities give teens an alternative to drug addiction.

in these groups are at risk of abusing drugs. The Reality

Check for Indigenous People program tries to scare kids

away from drug use. Program workers take the kids to

places where drug addicts live. With their own eyes, kids

see the poor conditions. They see the dangerous living

areas. On one field trip, a sick, homeless addict named Angela came up to the kids and told them, "Don't end up here." Angela was a good lesson about not using drugs.

If you have a problem, don't use drugs to feel better. Talk about it with someone you respect. This can include parents, teachers, or school counselors. Grandparents, ministers, and youth group leaders are also people you can turn to for support. Talking to someone who cares is a good way to prevent drug abuse.

Smart kids make informed choices. They choose to be healthy and not to abuse drugs.

How can you tell if someone you know is using drugs? Experts say the way people look or act often changes when they use drugs. Here are some signs to look for:
- Changing friends (to hang out with kids who use drugs)
- Sleeping a lot (maybe even in class)
- Losing interest in school
- Having red or puffy eyes
- Gaining or losing weight
- Becoming moody, angry, cranky, or worried all the time

GLOSSARY

addiction (uh DIK shun) dependence on something to feel normal or good; the need for a substance that is habit-forming

drug abuse (drug ub YOOSS) the use of any drug, legal or illegal, in a way that is not prescribed or recommended

drug treatment center (drug TREET ment SEN tur) a clinic or other medical facility where people are admitted to get over drug abuse. Often the patient must stay at the center 24 hours a day for several weeks or months.

DXM (dee ex em) the chemical dextromethorphan, a common ingredient in cough syrup. In high doses, DXM can make users feel high or drunk, and is known to cause allergic reactions.

halfway house a place for people to live as they recover from drug abuse. Residents of a halfway house follow house rules and sleep at the house each night, but they adjust to the real world by going to school, to work, or out with friends and family during the day.

hallucinate (huh LOO sin ate) to see, hear, or experience something that isn't really there

huffing inhaling the fumes of chemicals or other substances to get high

over-the-counter drugs medicines, such as aspirin and cough syrup, that can be bought in stores without a prescription

prescription drugs (pre SKRIP shun drugs) drugs authorized by a doctor for medical use. The doctor prescribes the medicine, and a pharmacist is then allowed to sell it to the patient. Prescription drugs are to be used in a certain dose for a certain length of time.

recreational drugs (rek ree AY shun ul drugs) drugs used without a medical reason, to alter mood or perception

For More Information

Books

Lishak, Antony. *Drugs*. North Mankato, MN: Smart Apple Media, 2007.

Orr, Tamra B. *Ecstasy*. New York: Rosen Central, 2008.

Parks, Peggy J. *Driving Under the Influence*. Yankton, SD: Erickson, 2007.

Sommers, Michael A. *Cocaine*. New York: Rosen Central, 2008.

Stewart, Gail B. *Smoking*. Yankton, SD: Erickson, 2007.

Web Sites

Check Yourself
http://checkyourself.com/
At this site sponsored by the Partnership for a Drug-Free America,
young people can read true stories about drug use, find accurate drug
information, and take quizzes to check their risk of trouble.

D.A.R.E. America for Kids
www.dare.com/kids/index_3.htm
Informative games, tips, and puzzles from the official site of the Drug Abuse Resistance
Education program, currently used in 75 percent of U.S. school districts and 41 countries.

deal.org
www.deal.org
Affiliated with the Royal Canadian Mounted Police, this site addresses important
issues affecting Canadian youth, including drugs and drug abuse.

Neuroscience for Kids
http://faculty.washington.edu/chudler/alco.html

University of Washington, Seattle, researchers explain to kids how different drugs
affect the brain and body. Start with Alcohol, and click the links at the bottom of the
page to learn about inhalants, marijuana, cocaine, ecstasy, and much more.

INDEX

ABOUT THE AUTHOR

Toney Allman holds degrees from Ohio State University and the University of Hawaii. She lives in rural Virginia, where she enjoys gardening, reading, and learning about the natural world. She has written more than two dozen nonfiction books for students and learned something new and fun from every one of them.